I0810848

YOUR FAVORITE STARS

FEATURING CRISTIANO RONALDO

FACTS, QUIZZES, ACTIVITIES, AND MORE!

by Erin Falligant

CAPSTONE PRESS
a capstone imprint

This is an unauthorized biography.

Published by Capstone Press, an imprint of Capstone
1710 Roe Crest Drive, North Mankato, Minnesota 56003
capstonepub.com

Copyright © 2026 by Capstone. All rights reserved. No part of this publication may be reproduced in whole or in part, or stored in a retrieval system, or transmitted in any form or by any means, electronic, mechanical, photocopying, recording, or otherwise, without written permission of the publisher.

Library of Congress Cataloging-in-Publication Data is available on the Library of Congress website.
ISBN: 9798875254963 (hardcover)
ISBN: 9798875254918 (paperback)
ISBN: 9798875254925 (ebook PDF)

Summary: A collection of fun facts, quizzes, and activities featuring the soccer superstar Cristiano Ronaldo.

Editorial Credits
Editor: Carrie Sheely; Designers: Elijah Blue and Heidi Thompson;
Media Researcher: Rebekah Hubstenberger; Production Specialist: Tori Abraham

Image Credits
Alamy: PA Images/Jon Buckle, 37, Retro AdArchives, 33; Associated Press: Paulo Duarte, 18, Albanian Prime Minster Office, 43; Getty Images: Alex Caparros, 15, Alex Grimm, 21, CR7 Footwear, 29, Emilio Andreoli, 16, Francois Nel, cover, Gonzalo Arroyo Moreno, 8-9, Handout/CR7 Play It Cool, 31, Hulton Archive, 40, Jan Kruger, 14, Kevin C. Cox, 34, Lars Baron, 23, Naomi Baker, 7, Octavio Passos, 5, 45, Pedro Loureiro/Eurasia Sport Images, 17 (middle left), Rafal Oleksiewicz, 26-27, 46-47, Rich Storry, 11 (left), Thananuwat Srirasant, 24, Tullio M. Puglia, 39, Yasser Bakhsh, 19, 25, 44; Shutterstock: ANNA ZASIMOVA (rainbow chrome star), back cover and throughout, Brovko Serhii (soccer ball), cover, 8-9, 17, 40, Christos Georghiou, 22 (soccer player silhouette), derter (chrome sparkle), back cover and throughout, em_concepts, cover (Portugal flag), Hampus design, 6, inCube_graphics, 35, ivector, 30 (middle right), Lauritta, cover (soccer trophy), Mashaart (silver star), back cover and throughout, Nattawit Khomsanit, 32, Only _up, 30 (middle left), Stefan Constantin 22, 11 (right), 41, Tartila, 42, Viktoria Kazakova, 30 (bottom), v_kulieva (blurry heart background), cover and throughout, Yuliia Sobolieva (blue sparkle), 17, 43

Any additional websites and resources referenced in this book are not maintained, authorized, or sponsored by Capstone. All product and company names are trademarks™ or registered® trademarks of their respective holders.

*Stats are current through February 2025.

Printed and bound in China. 006461

TABLE OF

CONTENTS

CHAPTER 1

LUCKY NUMBER 7

Is **CRISTIANO RONALDO** considered one of the greatest soccer players of all time? Siu! (That's "yes" in Portuguese, his native language.) He has scored more goals than any other player in men's international soccer. He also has more than 1 billion followers on social media, making him one of the most popular athletes on the planet!

Cristiano has the nickname CR7. It combines his initials with his favorite jersey number. For most of his career, he has worn jersey number 7, which is considered lucky. But with his skills and confidence, Ronaldo doesn't need luck. He makes things happen through hard work and dedication to his sport.

STAR SCOOP!

Ronaldo wasn't sure he was ready to wear number 7 for Manchester United. He was still a teenager, and number 7 had belonged to superstar David Beckham. But Ronaldo's manager convinced him he was good enough—and the rest is history!

quiz!

TEST YOUR RONALDO KNOWLEDGE

How well do you know Ronaldo? Which of these are true and which are false?

1. Ronaldo has played for five different countries: Portugal, England, Spain, Italy, and Saudi Arabia.

2. In Spain, his nickname is "El Bicho."

3. Ronaldo has been ranked the world's highest-paid athlete.

4. He has played for Real Madrid and Manchester City.

5. Ronaldo usually plays the position of defender.

6. He is known for his jumping skills, which help him score headers.

7. He is 6 feet, 2 inches (183 centimeters) tall, which is considered tall for a soccer player.

Answers: 1. T, 2. T—It means "The Bug.", 3. T, 4. F—He played for Real Madrid and Manchester United., 5. F—He is a forward., 6. T, 7. T

TROPHY CASE

Ronaldo's trophy case is full! See how many times he won each of these awards.

Best FIFA Men's Player—3

FIFA Club World Cup Winner—4

UEFA Best Player in Europe—4

Golden Boot (for scoring)—4

Champions League Winner—5

Ballon d'Or (for best player) — 5

Ronaldo poses with his five Ballon d'Or trophies.

STAR SCOOP!

Ronaldo accepted his fifth Ballon d'Or award halfway up the Eiffel Tower in Paris! The trophy was awarded by *France Football* magazine at one of France's most popular sites.

TOUGHEST RIVAL

Who has been considered Ronaldo's biggest rival? That's superstar forward **LIONEL MESSI**. Ronaldo and Messi are considered the two best soccer players of their generation. Fans and sportscasters disagree about which player is better. Ronaldo has scored more goals and hat tricks (three goals in one game), but Messi has won more trophies and awards. However the stats stack up, these two players have pushed and challenged each other for nearly 20 years.

STAR SCOOP!

Messi has said that he and Ronaldo weren't rivals at all. But Ronaldo says the competition has been "a healthy rivalry that spectators liked a lot. Whoever likes Cristiano Ronaldo doesn't have to hate Messi or vice versa." Good attitude, Ronaldo!

TeamViewer

CHAPTER 2

MEMORABLE MOMENTS

BY THE HUNDREDS

WHEN DID RONALDO SCORE EACH OF THESE MILESTONE GOALS?

100TH (for Manchester United): January 2008 in a penalty kick against Tottenham

200TH (for Real Madrid): December 2010 against Valencia

300TH (for Real Madrid): May 2012, only 17 months after his 200th goal

400TH (for Real Madrid): January 2014, a goal he dedicated to Portuguese soccer player Eusébio

500TH (for Real Madrid): September 2015 against Malmo

600TH (for Real Madrid): June 2017 to win the Champions League final

700TH (for Portugal): October 2019 against Ukraine

800TH (for Manchester United): December 2021 against Arsenal

900TH (for Portugal): September 2024 against Croatia

WILL HE REACH 1,000? NEVER BET AGAINST RONALDO!

HAT TRICK HISTORY

Ronaldo scored his first hat trick in 2008, and he's never stopped. Ronaldo was the first player to score **10** hat tricks in men's international football. In 2014, he sent his home country, Portugal, to the World Cup by scoring a hat trick. And sometimes, three goals in one game just wasn't enough. In 2015, while playing for Real Madrid, Ronaldo scored five goals in a game—twice!

Ronaldo scoring his fifth goal in a game in September 2015

66

STAR SCOOP!

By the end of 2024, Ronaldo had scored 66 hat tricks. That's more than any other pro player in the history of soccer.

WOW-WORTHY GOALS

April 2009

A 40-yard strike that earned Ronaldo a Puskas Award for the "most beautiful" goal of the year

May 2014

A back-heel goal pulled off when he wasn't even facing the net

January 2016

A perfect hat trick—one right-footed goal, one left-footed goal, and one header

April 2018

A jaw-dropping bicycle kick with his foot over 7.5 feet (2.3 meters) off the ground

December 2019

A header for the match-winning goal

December 2023

A header in the 92nd minute of the match

November 2024

Another bicycle kick performed only two months shy of his 40th birthday

STAR SCOOP!

Ronaldo's bicycle kick goal in 2018 earned him a standing ovation—from the other team! The defender for the opposing team called it a "PlayStation goal" because it was performed with perfect technique.

BOUNCING BACK

Not all of Ronaldo's memorable moments were positive. In 2008, he tore a ligament in his ankle that kept him sidelined for 94 days. Other times, he made the news because of disagreements with teammates or coaches. After the 2006 World Cup, he was booed by fans. He had demanded a red card for Wayne Rooney, a player who was his teammate during the regular season. But whatever the setback, he always keeps going.

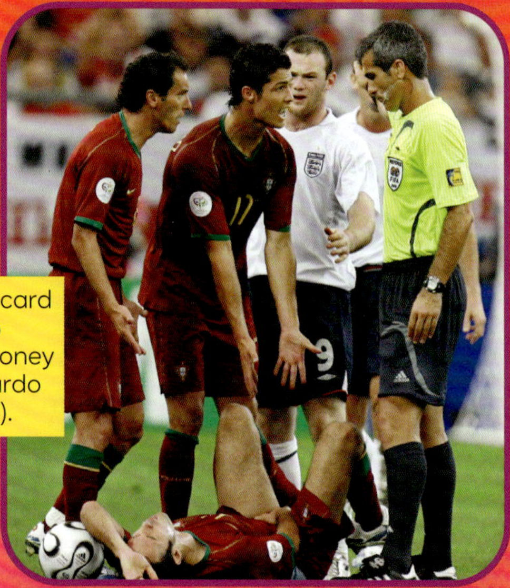

Ronaldo wanted a red card for Rooney at the 2006 World Cup because Rooney stepped on player Ricardo Carvalho (lying on field).

STAR SCOOP!

Ronaldo believes that it's actually good to have problems because it's the only way to get better as a person and as a player. He once said, "I learn the most when I'm down."

Ronaldo on the field with an injury in August 2023

CHAPTER 3

THE WAY HE PLAYS

For most of his career, Ronaldo has played a **forward**, which is also known as a striker or an attacker. This player's main job is to score goals. Ronaldo uses his speed, strength, and jumping ability to get the job done. Ronaldo is also good at moving around the field in a way that pulls defenders out of position, making it easier to score. He is right-handed and usually kicks with his right foot, but he's a strong striker with both feet.

STAR SCOOP!

Out of 900 goals, Ronaldo scored 178 of them with his left foot—and another 153 of them with his head!

STOJANOVIĆ
20

RONALDO'S SUPER SKILLS

What makes Ronaldo so fun to watch? His skills and tricks on the field, like . . .

DRIBBLING: MOVING THE BALL WITH HIS FEET

THE STEP-OVER: A QUICK FOOT MOVEMENT THAT TRICKS OPPONENTS SO HE CAN DRIBBLE PAST

THE ELASTICO OR FLIP-FLAP: QUICKLY MOVING THE BALL FROM ONE SIDE OF HIS BODY TO THE OTHER

THE ROULETTE: CIRCLING THE BALL AROUND HIS FOOT TO CHANGE DIRECTION

BICYCLE KICKS: KICKING THE BALL BACKWARD OVER HIS HEAD WHILE DOING A SOMERSAULT IN THE AIR

VOLLEY KICKS: KICKING THE BALL IN THE AIR TO SHOOT OR PASS

HEADERS: SCORING OR PASSING BY HITTING THE BALL OFF HIS FOREHEAD

PENALTY KICKS: A FREE SHOT AT THE GOAL AWARDED AFTER HE HAS BEEN FOULED

BACKHEEL PASSES: KICKING THE BALL BACKWARD WITH HIS HEEL

THE KNUCKLEBALL: KICKING THE BALL WHILE CREATING VERY LITTLE SPIN

STAR SCOOP!

Ronaldo even has a skill named after him: the "Ronaldo chop." He uses it to quickly change direction while dribbling toward a defender. How? He puts one foot in front of the ball while swinging the other behind to kick diagonally.

SIUUU!

No one celebrates quite like Ronaldo after scoring. He runs toward the camera and circles his hand to tell the crowd to get ready. Then he jumps—the kind of **incredible leap** that helps him score headers—and spins in the air. He lands with his arms spread wide while shouting "siuuu!" (or "yesss!"). He first performed the siu during a preseason game in 2013. Now it's one of the most famous and **most copied** celebrations in sports!

STAR SCOOP!

Ronaldo made up his celebration on the spot after scoring a goal. He said, "It just came out. It was just natural, to be honest. Since that, I started to do it more often and I feel like the supporters and the fans see it and they're like, 'Cristiano, siiiiiuuuu!'"

MAKE A CELEBRATION

You can make up your own celebration! Try to include at least three moves and one word or phrase. Give it a name, and then teach it to a friend. Or make up a celebration together! With two people, you can include a high five, fist bump, or special handshake. Here are ideas to make your celebration stand out!

PHYSICAL MOVES SUCH AS...

- a dance move
- a martial arts kick
- crossing your arms at your chest
- a pose you can strike and hold at the end
- pretending to shoot an arrow with a bow
- a hand gesture, like saluting your fans, making a heart with your hands, or pointing toward the sky

POLONIA/PORTUGAL
12 OUTUBRO 2024
VARSOVIA

CHAPTER 4

PARTNERS, BUSINESS, AND BRANDS

Ronaldo is as successful in business as he is in soccer. In 2024, he earned $260 million, and almost a fifth of that came from business projects off the field! He has partnered with big brands like **Nike**, launched his own YouTube channel, and created his own fashion brand called **CR7**. He also created an app called **Erakulis** that tracks fitness and nutrition. Whenever Ronaldo decides to hang up his soccer cleats, he'll have plenty of other interests to keep him busy.

Ronaldo with CR7 footwear

STAR SCOOP!

In 2024, *Forbes* magazine declared Ronaldo the highest-paid soccer player in the world—for the sixth time in 10 years!

RONALDO'S CR7 BRAND INCLUDES:

- UNDERWEAR
- LOUNGEWEAR AND PAJAMAS
- SOCKS
- BATHROBES
- EIGHT DIFFERENT FRAGRANCES (INCLUDING "GAME ON" AND "PLAY IT COOL")
- KIDS' CLOTHING SUCH AS PAJAMAS, SOCKS, AND UNDERWEAR

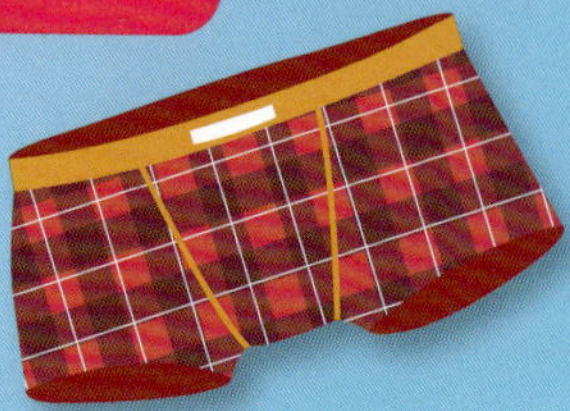

STAR SCOOP!

Although Ronaldo helps design clothes for his CR7 brand, he urges people to make their own fashion statements. "Individuality for me has always been important," he has said, "and I would certainly encourage people to follow their own path."

PARTNERING UP

Companies know that having Ronaldo's name or face in their ads is a great way to boost sales. In 2016, Ronaldo signed a lifetime partnership with Nike worth as much as $1 billion! He was only the third athlete to be signed for life, after basketball superstars Michael Jordan and LeBron James. Ronaldo has also partnered with brands including Armani, Tag Heuer watches, **Clear** shampoo, and **Herbalife**. What kinds of brands does Ronaldo back up? Brands that support his favorite things: fashion, fitness, and wellness.

DON'T CRACK UNDER PRESSURE
TAG Heuer
SWISS AVANT-GARDE SINCE 1860
AQUARACER CALIBRE 5
Cristiano Ronaldo is born to break all the records. His motivation is to win at every occasion to challenge the human statistics. Like TAG Heuer, Ronaldo surpasses the limits of his field and never cracks under pressure.
WWW.TAGHEUER.CO.UK

Nike designed more than 30 pairs of cleats for Ronaldo. Each pair was created to tell Ronaldo's story and honor his accomplishments.

The Safari had an animal print to celebrate his speed.

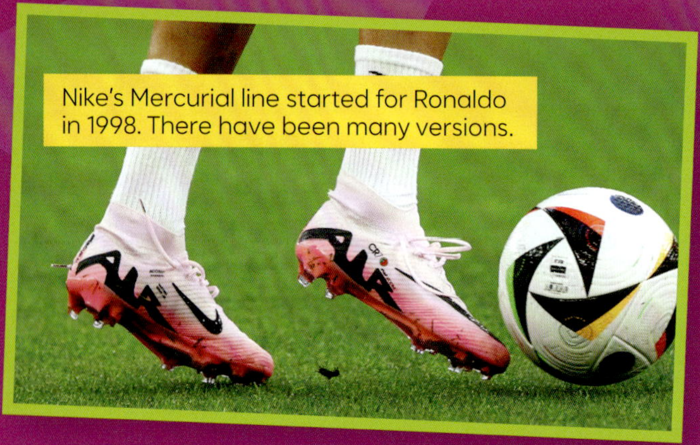

Nike's Mercurial line started for Ronaldo in 1998. There have been many versions.

The Galaxy featured a path of seven stars.

Others showcased his name or the number of goals he'd scored.

DESIGN YOUR OWN CLEATS

How would your cleats look? Design cleats that tell your unique story!

1. Trace the outline of a shoe onto paper.
2. What are your favorite team colors? What patterns feel most like you—stars, stripes, animal prints, or polka dots?
3. Add numbers, words, or phrases that have special meaning.
4. Give your shoe a signature name. Voilà!

CHAPTER **5**

FANS AND FAMILY

In 2021, Ronaldo became the first person in the world to reach 500 million followers across Instagram, Facebook, and Twitter (now known as X). By the end of 2024, only three years later, that number had grown to 923 million followers. Ronaldo also launched his own YouTube channel called UR Cristiano. It took only 90 minutes for him to attract more than 1 million subscribers, setting a YouTube record! When Ronaldo has something to say, post, or share, people tune in.

STAR SCOOP!

Ronaldo was once a fan boy too! He admired two Brazilian soccer stars who happened to have names similar to his: Ronaldo Nazario and Ronaldinho. He said, "I have great respect for them. I grew up watching them play."

Ronaldo and Ronaldinho

quiz!

FAMILY FACTS

Which of these do you think are true about Ronaldo's family?

1. Ronaldo was the oldest of four kids.

2. His family was quite wealthy.

3. Ronaldo shared a room with his brother and two sisters growing up.

4. The family lived in a small home with a tin roof overlooking the ocean.

5. His mom worked part-time for a soccer club in Portugal.

6. Ronaldo struggled in school, and his parents let him quit at age 14 to focus on soccer.

7. His dad passed away when Ronaldo was only 20.

8. Ronaldo has five children of his own.

Answers: 1. False—He was the youngest., 2. False—They had very little money., 3. True, 4. True, 5. False—That was his dad., 6. True, 7. True, 8. True

Ronaldo with his mother

STAR SCOOP!

Ronaldo prioritizes his family. He is very close to his mother, Maria. He is grateful for her constant support and how it has helped make him successful.

WHAT'S IN A NAME?

Ronaldo's full name is Cristiano Ronaldo dos Santos Aveiro. Why does he have two last names? Because dos Santos was his mother's last name and Aveiro was his father's. The name "Ronaldo" was a nod to one of his dad's favorite actors, U.S. President Ronald Reagan. Reagan was an actor long before he became president. Both Ronald and Ronaldo seemed destined for greatness, so maybe there is something in a name!

Ronald Reagan

STAR SCOOP!

Ronaldo's mom is well known on social media. She has more than 4 million followers on Instagram!

CHAPTER 6

RONALDO'S LEGACY

Ronaldo has donated millions of dollars to help others, including victims of natural disasters and the COVID-19 pandemic. He cares deeply about children's health. Ronaldo raised money for kids battling leukemia and for childhood cancer treatment centers in Portugal. He once paid for a 10-month-old boy to get brain surgery. Ronaldo also auctioned off his prized **2013 Ballon d'Or trophy** to raise money for Make-a-Wish. This organization grants wishes to children with life-threatening illnesses.

Ronaldo and soccer player Gianluigi Buffon pose with two children who were injured in the 2019 Albanian earthquake.

STAR SCOOP!

In 2015, Ronaldo was named the world's most charitable sportsperson by DoSomething, an organization that inspires young people to take action.

7 THINGS NAMED AFTER #7

1. THE CRISTIANO RONALDO INTERNATIONAL AIRPORT ON THE PORTUGUESE ISLAND WHERE HE WAS BORN

2. THE CR7 MUSEUM IN MADEIRA THAT DISPLAYS HIS TROPHIES

3. PESTANA CR7 LIFESTYLE HOTELS IN EUROPE AND THE U.S.

4. A GALAXY NAMED COSMOS REDSHIFT 7 (CR7) DISCOVERED IN 2015

5. **THE CRISTIANO RONALDO ACADEMY, A SOCCER TRAINING FACILITY IN PORTUGAL**

6. **CR7 FITNESS BY CRUNCH GYMS IN SPAIN AND PORTUGAL**

7. **BABIES!**

CR7 Museum

STAR SCOOP!

As of late 2022, "Ronaldo" was the second most popular baby name inspired by a soccer star. The first was "Salah," inspired by pro player Mohamed Salah Ghaly.

WISE WORDS

Ronaldo has learned a thing or two during his journey to success. So when he speaks, we listen!

"If you think you're perfect already, then you never will be."

"I don't have to show anything to anyone. There is nothing to prove."

"I don't mind people hating me, because it pushes me."

"I think sometimes the best training is to rest."

"We cannot live being obsessed with what other people think about us. It's impossible to live like that."

"It is my conviction that there are no limits to learning, and that it can never stop, no matter what our age."

"I feel an endless need to learn, to improve, to evolve, not only to please the coach and fans, but also to feel satisfied with myself."

"I'm not going to change the world. You're not going to change the world. But we can help—we can all help."

ABOUT THE AUTHOR

Erin Falligant has written more than 50 books for children. Her Joss series for American Girl, written about a young surfer with hearing loss, earned a 2020 Moonbeam Gold Medal Award. Erin draws from her master's degree in child clinical psychology to write advice books on changing bodies, standing up to bullies, making friends, and mastering mindfulness. To learn more about Erin and her books, visit www.erinfalligant.com

READ MORE ABOUT YOUR FAVORITE STARS!

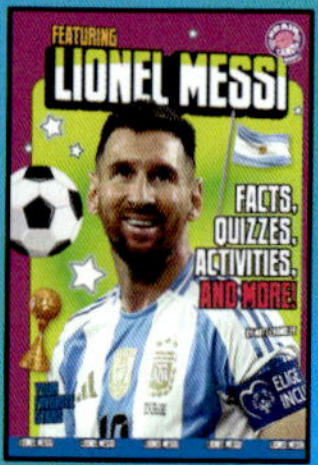